George Ticknor Curtis

# An ORATION

delivered on the Fourth of July 1862, before the Municipal Authorities of the City

of Boston

George Ticknor Curtis

**An ORATION**
*delivered on the Fourth of July 1862, before the Municipal Authorities of the City of Boston*

ISBN/EAN: 9783741123610

Manufactured in Europe, USA, Canada, Australia, Japa

Cover: Foto ©Suzi / pixelio.de

Manufactured and distributed by brebook publishing software (www.brebook.com)

George Ticknor Curtis

# An ORATION

AN

# ORATION

DELIVERED ON THE

## FOURTH OF JULY, 1862,

BEFORE

# THE MUNICIPAL AUTHORITIES

OF THE

## CITY OF BOSTON.

### BY GEORGE TICKNOR CURTIS.

———————•••———————

BOSTON:

J. E. FARWELL AND COMPANY, PRINTERS TO THE CITY,

No. 37 CONGRESS STREET.

1862.

# CITY OF BOSTON.

*In Board of Aldermen,* July 7, 1862.

ORDERED: That the thanks of the City Council are hereby presented to the HON. GEORGE T. CURTIS for his very eloquent and patriotic Oration before the Municipal Authorities of the City of Boston on the occasion of the Eighty-sixth Anniversary of the Declaration of the Independence of the United States of America, and that he be requested to furnish a copy for publication.

Passed: Sent down for concurrence.

THOMAS P. RICH, *Chairman.*

*In Common Council,* July 10, 1862.

Concurred.

JOSHUA D. BALL, *President.*

Approved, July 11, 1862.

JOSEPH M. WIGHTMAN, *Mayor.*

A true copy.

Attest: SAMUEL F. McCLEARY, *City Clerk.*

# ORATION.

Had I felt at liberty to consult my own inclination alone, I should have asked you to excuse me from taking part in the proceedings of this day. At a much earlier period of life, I enjoyed the distinction of being placed on the long roll of those who have successively spoken to the people of Boston, at the bidding of their municipal authorities, on this our national anniversary. At this particular juncture, I could well have desired to be spared from the performance of any such public duty. I had prepared myself to bear what is now upon us, in silence and obscurity ; doing the infinitely little that I may, to alleviate personal suffering, sustaining the hopes of those who are nearest to me, and endeavoring to cherish in my own breast a living faith in the strength and perpetuity of our republican forms of government.

But private wishes are nothing — private tastes are nothing — in the presence of great public trials and dangers. We cannot, if we would, escape the responsibilities which such trials and dangers entail upon us. If we fly to the uttermost parts of the earth, the thought of our country is with us there. If we put on the robes of the stoic, or wrap ourselves in the philosophy of the fatalist, the heart beneath will beat for the land of our birth, in spite of the outward man. There is no peace, there is no hope, there is no happiness, in a state of indifference to the welfare and honor of our country. The most sordid of men, whose sole delight consists in laying, day by day, one more piece of gold on his already swollen heaps, has no more assured rest from anxiety for his country, in times of real peril, than he whose whole being quivers beneath the blows which public disasters or disgraces inflict upon a refined and sensitive nature. To love our country; to labor for its prosperity and repose : to contend, in civil life, for the measures which we believe essential to its good; to yearn for that long, deep, tranquil flow of public affairs, which we fondly hope is to reach and bear safely on its bosom those in whom we are to have an earthly hereafter ; these are the nobler passions and the higher aims which distinguish the civilized from the savage man. Even if I did not feel such emotions deeply, how could I bring here at such a time as this the doubts and

misgivings of one fearful for himself? The thickly
crowding memories of the far-off dead, who have
fallen in the bitter contests of this civil war, admon-
ish me of the insignificance of such fears. Who shall
bring a thought of the exertions, the sacrifices or the
responsibilities of public discourse into the presence
of the calamities of his country!

I am here for a far other purpose. I come to plead
for the Constitution of our country. I am here to
show you, from my own earnest convictions, how dan-
gerous it may be to forego all care for the connection
between the political past and the political future. I
am here to state to you, as I have read them on the
page of history, the fundamental conditions on which
alone, as I believe, the people of these States can be
a nation, and preserve their liberties. I am here to
endeavor to rescue the idea of union from heresies as
destructive as the disorganizing and justly reprobated
heresies of secession. I wish to do what I can to
define to rational and intelligent minds the real nature and limits of the national supremacy; and to
vindicate it from the corroding influence of doctrines
which are leading us away from the political faith
and precepts of a free people.

Do you say that there is no need of such a discus-
sion? Reflect for a moment, I pray you, on what has
already crept into the common uses of our political

speech. We hear men talk about the "old" Constitution; as if that admirable frame of government, which is not yet older than some who still live under its sway, and which has bestowed on this nation a vigor unexampled in history, were already in its decrepitude; or as if it had become suspended from its functions by general consent, to await at respectful distance the advent of some new authority, as yet unknown. We hear men talk of the "old" Union; as if there were a choice about the terms on which the Union can subsist, or as if those terms were not to be taken as having been fixed, on the day on which Washington and his compatriots signed the Constitution of the United States. You will not say that this tendency — this apparent willingness to break away from the past and its obligations, and to throw ourselves upon a careless tempting of the future — does not demand your sober consideration. I beg you also to call before you another symptom of these unsettled times. With an extravagance partly habitual to us, and partly springing from the intense exertions of the year which has just passed, we have encountered the doctrines of secession and disunion with many theories about the national unity and the Federal authority, which are not founded in history or in law. Are you not conscious that there has been poured forth from hundreds of American pulpits, platforms, and presses, and on the floors of Congress, a species of what is called argument, in defence of the national supremacy, which ill befits the nature of our republican institutions? When I hear one of these courtier-like preachers or writers, for our American sovereigns, resting the authority of our government on a doctrine that might have gained him promotion at the hands of James or Charles Stuart, I cannot help wishing that he had lived in an age when such teachings, if not actually believed to be sound, were at all events exceedingly useful to the teachers. My friends, I cannot bear the thought of vindicating the supremacy of our national government by anything but the just title on which it was founded; and I will not desert the solid ground of our republican constitutional liberty for any purpose on earth while there is a hope of maintaining it.

I know of no just foundation for the title of government in this country, but consent — that consent which resides in compact, contract, stipulation, concession — the "*do et concedo*" of public grants. Give me a solemn cession of political sovereign powers, evidenced by a public transaction and a public charter, and you have given me a civil contract, to which I can apply the rules of public law and the obligations of justice between man and man; on which I can separate the legitimate powers of the government

2

from the rights of the people; on which I can, with
perfect propriety, assert the authority of law in the
halls of criminal jurisprudence, or, if need be, at the
mouth of the cannon. But when you speak of any
other right of one collection of people or States to
govern another collection of people or States; when
you go beyond a public charter to create a national
unity and a duty of loyalty and submission independent of that charter; when you undertake to found
government on something not embraced by a grant —
I understand you to employ a language and ideas
that ought never to be uttered by an American
tongue, and which, if carried out in practice, will
put an end to the principles on which your liberties
are founded.

For these and many other reasons — most appropriate for our consideration this day — let us recur to
certain indisputable facts in our history. I shall
make no apology for insisting on the precedents of
our national history. No nation can safely lay aside
the teachings, the obligations, or the facts of its pre-
vious existence. You cannot make a *tabula rasa* of
your political condition, and write upon it a purely
original system, with no traditions, no law, no com-
pacts, no beliefs, no limitations, derived from the gen-
erations who have gone before you, without ruinously
failing to improve. Revolutionary France tried such

a proceeding ; — and property, life, religion, morals, public order and public tranquillity went down into a confusion no better than barbarism, out of which society could be raised again only by the strong hand of a despot. WE are of a race which ought to have learned by the experience of a thousand years, that reforms, improvements, progress, must be conducted with a fixed reference to those antecedent facts which have already formed the chief condition of the national existence. Let us attend to some of the well known truths in our history.

1. The Declaration of Independence was not accepted by the people of the colonies, and their Delegates in Congress were not authorized to enter into a Union, without a reservation to the people of each colony of its distinct separate right of internal self-government. To represent the abstract sentiments of the Declaration as inconsistent with any law or institution existing in any one of the colonies, is to contradict the record and history of its adoption. What, for example, do you make of the following resolution of the people of Maryland in convention, adopted on the 28th day of June, 1776, and laid before the Continental Congress three days before the Declaration of Independence was signed : " That the deputies of said Colony or any three or more of them, be authorized and empowered to concur with

the other United Colonies, or a majority of them,
in declaring the United Colonies free and independent States ; in forming such further compact and
confederation between them ; in making foreign alli-
ances, and in adopting such other measures as shall
be adjudged necessary for securing the liberties of
America ; and, that said Colony will hold itself
bound by the resolutions of the majority of the
United Colonies, in the premises : *provided*, THE SOLE
AND EXCLUSIVE RIGHT OF REGULATING THE INTERNAL
GOVERNMENT AND POLICE OF THAT COLONY BE RESERVED
TO THE PEOPLE THEREOF."

This annunciation of the sense and purpose in
which the people of Maryland accepted the Declaration, is just as much a part of the record as the
Declaration itself ; and it clearly controls for them
the meaning and application of every political ax-
iom or principle which the Declaration contains. It
was intended to signify to the country and the
world, that the people of Maryland consented to
separate themselves from the sovereignty of Great
Britain, *on the condition*, that the right to maintain
within their own limits just such a system of society and government as they might see fit to maintain, should belong to them, *notwithstanding* anything said in the Declaration to which they were
asked to give their assent.

Several of the other colonies made a similar express reservation; and all of them. and all the people of America, understood that every colony accepted the Declaration, in fact, in the same sense. No man in the whole country, from the 4th of July, 1776, to the adoption of the Articles of Confederation, ever supposed that the Revolutionary Congress acquired any legal right to interfere with the domestic concerns of any one of the colonies which then became States, or any moral authority to lay down rules for determining what laws, institutions, or customs, or what condition of its inhabitants, should be adopted or continued by the States in their internal government. From that day to this, it has ever been a received doctrine of American law, that the Revolutionary Congress exercised, with the assent of the whole people, certain powers which were needful for the common defence ; but that these powers in no way touched or involved the sovereign right of each State to regulate its own internal condition.

2. When the Articles of Confederation were finally ratified, in 1781, there was placed in the very front of the instrument the solemn declaration that, "Each State retains its sovereignty, freedom, and independence, and every power. jurisdiction. and right, which is not by this Confederation expressly

delegated to the United States in Congress assembled;" and the powers given to the United States in Congress related exclusively to those affairs in which the States had a common concern, and were framed with a view to the common defence against a foreign enemy, in order to secure, by joint exertions, the independence and sovereignty of each of the States.

3. When the Constitution of the United States was finally established, in 1788, the people of each State, acting through authorized agents, executed, by a resolution or other public act, a cession of certain sovereign powers, described in the Constitution, to the Government which that Constitution provided to receive and exercise them. These powers being once absolutely granted by public instruments duly executed in behalf of the people of each State, were thenceforth incapable of being resumed; for I hold that there is nothing in the nature of political powers which renders them, when absolutely ceded, any more capable of being resumed at pleasure by the grantors, than a right of property is when once conveyed by an absolute deed. In both cases, those who receive the grant hold under a contract; and if that contract, as is the case with the Constitution, provides for a common arbiter to determine its meaning and operation, there is no resulting right in the

parties, from the instrument itself, to determine any question that arises under it.

At the same time, it is never to be forgotten that the powers and rights of separate internal government which were not ceded by the people of the States, or which they did not by adopting the Constitution agree to restrain, remained in the people of each State in full sovereignty. It might have been enough for their safety to have rested upon this as a familiarly understood and well defined principle of public law, implied in every such grant. But the people did not see fit to trust to implication alone. They insisted upon annexing to the Constitution an amendment, which declares that "The powers not delegated to the United States by the Constitution, nor prohibited by it to the States, are reserved to the States respectively, or to the people."

We thus see that, from the first dawn of our national existence, through every form which it has yet assumed, a dual character has constantly attended our political condition. A nation has existed, because there has all along existed a central authority having the right to prescribe the rule of action for the whole people, on certain subjects, occasions, and relations. In this sense and in no other, to this extent but no farther, we have been since

1776, and are now, a nation. At the beginning, the limits of this central authority, in respect to which we are a nation, were defined by general popular understanding; but more recently they were fixed in written terms and public charters, first by the Articles of Confederation, and ultimately and with a more enlarged scope and a more efficient machinery, by the Constitution. The latter instrument made this central authority a government proper, but with limited and defined powers, which are supreme within their own appropriate sphere. In like manner, from the beginning, there has existed another political body; — distinct, sovereign within its own sphere, and independent as to all the powers and objects of government not ceded or restrained under the Federal Constitution. This body is the State; a political corporation, of which each inhabitant is a subject, as he is at the same time a subject of that other political corporation known as the United States.

All this is familiar to you. But I state it here, because I wish to remind you that the careful preservation of this separate political body, the State, — this sovereign right of self-government as far as it has been retained by the people of each State, — has ever been a cardinal rule of action with the American people, and with all their wisest states-

men, Northern and Southern, of every school of
politics. There have been great differences of opinion, and great controversies, respecting the dividing
line which separates, or ought to be held to separate, the National from the State powers. But no
American statesman has ever lived, at any former
period, who would have dared to confess a purpose
to crush the State sovereignties out of existence;
and no man can now confess such a wish, without
arousing a popular jealousy which will not slumber
even in a time of civil war and national commo-
tion.

What is the true secret of this undying popular
jealousy on the subject of the State rights? What
is it, that even now — when we are sending our
best blood to be poured out in defence of the true
principle of the national supremacy — causes all
men who are not mad with some revolutionary project, to shrink from measures that appear to threaten
the integrity of State authority, and to pray that at
least that bitter and dreaded cup may pass from us?
It is the original, inborn and indestructible belief
that the preservation of the State sovereignty, within
its just and legitimate sphere, is essential to the
preservation of Republican liberty. Beyond a doubt,
it was this belief which led the people from the
first to object, as they sometimes did unreasonably

object, to the augmentation of the national powers. Perhaps they could not always explain — perhaps they did not always fully understand — all the grounds of this conviction. It has been, as it were, an instinct; and for one, I hope that instinct is as active and vigilant this day, as I am sure it was eighty years ago.

For I am persuaded that local self-government, to as great an extent as is consistent with national safety, is indispensable to the long continued existence of Republican government on a large scale. A Republic, in a great nation, demands those separate institutions, which imply in different portions of the nation some rights and powers with which no other portion of the nation can interfere. You may give the mere name of a Republic to a great many modes of national existence; but unless there are local privileges, immunities, and rights, that are not subject to the control of the national will, the government, although resting on a purely democratic basis, will be a despotism towards all the minorities. A great nation, too, that attempts republican government without such local institutions and rights, must soon lose even the republican form. Twice within the memory of some who are yet living, have the people of France tried the experiment of calling themselves a Republic; and France, be it remem-

bered, has been, ever since her great Revolution,
essentially a democratic country. But her republics
have never been anything but huge democracies,
acting with overwhelming force sometimes through
a head called a Directory, sometimes through a First
Consul, sometimes through a President, but ending
speedily in an Emperor and a Despotism. It is impracticable for a great and powerful democratic nation, whose power is not broken and checked by
local institutions of self-government, to avoid con-
ferring on its head and representative a large part
or the whole of its own unlimited force. If that
head is not clothed with such power, there will be
anarchy. Louis Napoleon, by the present theory of
French law, is the representative of the whole authority of the French nation — so constituted by
universal suffrage; and if his power did not in fact
correspond to this theory, order could not be pre-
served in France. The most skeptical person may
be convinced of this, who will read the Constitution
of the French Empire, remembering that it is the
work of the Emperor himself.

Turning now to our own country, let us suppose
that the States of this Union, from the Atlantic to
the Pacific, were obliterated to-day, and that the
people of this whole country were a consolidated
democracy, "one and indivisible." No laws would

then be made, no justice administered, no order
maintained, no institutions upheld, save in the name
and by the authority of the nation. What sort of a
Republic, think you, would that be? If it started
with the name and semblance, how long would it
preserve the substance of Republican institutions?
In order to act at all in the discharge of the vast
duties devolving upon it, the government of such a
Republic, extending over a country so enormous,
must more and more be made the depositary of the
irresistible force of the nation; and the theory that
the will of the government expresses in all cases the
will of the ruling majority, must soon confer upon
it that omnipotent power, beneath which minorities
and individuals can have no rights.

This is no mere speculation. Every reflecting man
in this country knows that he has some civil rights,
which he does not hold at the will and pleasure of
a majority of the people of the United States. He
knows that he holds these rights by a tenure which
cannot lawfully be touched by all the residue of the
nation. This is Republican liberty, as I understand
and value it; and without this principle in some
form of active and secure operation, I do not believe that any valuable Republican liberty is possible
in any great Democratic country on the face of
this earth. Certainly, it is not possible for us.

It seems to one who looks back upon our history, and who keeps before him the settled conditions of our liberty, almost impossible to believe that in consequence of a direct collision between the rightful supremacy of the nation and a wrongful assertion of State Sovereignty, we are exposed to all the evils of civil war, and to the danger of destroying the true principles of our system, in the effort to maintain them. That this danger is real and practical, will be conceded now, by every man who will contemplate the projects that spring up on all sides, looking to the acquisition of powers which have never belonged to the Federal Union by any theory under which it has yet existed. The main resemblance between these projects is that none of them will fit the known basis of the Constitution; and that as means, therefore, of curing the disorders of our country, or of making men obedient to the Constitution, their tendency is merely mischievous. At the same time, they are none of them founded on any theory of a new Union, or of a new form of national existence, which their authors can explain to us or to themselves. One man, for instance, wishes the government to assume the power of emancipating all the slaves of the South, by some decree, civil or military. But he cannot possibly explain what the government of the

Union is to be, when it has done this. Another man wants a sweeping confiscation of all the property of all the people of the revolted States, guilty and innocent alike. But he does not tell you what kind of a sovereign the United States is to be, after such a seizure shall have been consummated. A third, in addition to these things, and as if in imitation of the Austrian method of dealing with rebellious Hungary, wishes to declare a sweeping forfeiture of all political rights; an utter extinguishment of the corporate State existence, and a reduction of the people of the revolted States to a condition of military or some other vassalage. But he not only does not show how the Constitution enables the Federal Government to obliterate a State, but he does not even suggest what the Union is to be, when this is done, or even whence the requisite physical force is to be derived. Multitudes of politicians tell us that slavery is the root of all the national disasters, and that we must "strike at the root." But none of them tell us how we are to pass through these disasters to a safer condition, or what the condition is to be when we shall have "struck at the root."

Now it seems to me, endeavoring as I do to repress all merely vain and useless regrets for what is passed, and to find some safe principle of action

for the present and the future. that there is one
thought on which the people of the United States
should steadily fix their attention. We have seen
that our National Union has had three distinct
stages. The first was the Union formed by sending
delegates to the Revolutionary Congress, and by a
general submission to the measures adopted by that
body for the common defence. The second was the
closer league of the Confederation, the powers of
which were defined by a written charter. The third
was the institution of a government proper, with
sovereign but enumerated powers, under the Constitution. Now I infer from what I see of some of
the currents of public and private opinion, that
many persons entertain a vague expectation that the
military operations now necessarily carried on by the
Federal Government will result in the creation of
new civil relations, a new Union and a new Constitution of some kind, they know not what. He
would be a very bold and a very rash man, who
should undertake to predict what new constitution
can follow a civil war in a great country like this.
But looking back to the commencement of our national existence, we see that there never has been a
change in the form of the Union; there never has
been a new acquisition of political power by the
central government, which has been gained by force.

Such additions of foreign territory, as we have obtained by arms or treaty, have merely increased the area of the Union, but they have not augmented the political powers of the government in the smallest degree. The inhabitants of those regions have come into the Union subject to the same powers to which we, who were original parties to the formation of the Constitution, have always been subject, and to no others. The national authority has never gained the slightest increase of its political powers by force of arms. In every stage in which its powers have been augmented, the increase has been gained by the free, voluntary consent of the people of each State, without coercion of any kind.

This consideration certainly affords no reason why the Government of the United States should not vindicate its just authority under the Constitution, over the whole of its territory, by military power. The right of the Government of this Union to exercise the powers embraced in the Constitution rests, I repeat, upon a voluntary, irrevocable cession of those powers by the people of each State ; and no impartial publicist in the world will deny that the right to put down all military or other resistance to the exercise of those powers rests upon a just and perfect title. This title is founded on a public grant.

But when you come to the idea of acquiring

other and further powers by the exercise of force,
you come to a very different question. You then
have to consider whether a people whose civil polity
is founded on the title given by consent — who have
never known or admitted any other rule of action
than that expressed in the maxim that "govern-
ments derive their just powers from the consent of
the governed," — can proceed to found any new
political powers on a military conquest over a rebel-
lion, without changing the whole character of their
institutions. For my own part, with the best reflec-
tion I have been able to give to this momentous
subject, I have never been able to see how a majority of the American people can proceed to acquire
by military subjugation, or by military means, or
maxims, any *new* authority over the people or institutions of any State or class of States, without falling
back upon the same kind of title, as that by which
William of Normandy and his descendants acquired
and held the throne of England. That title was
founded on the sword.

Perhaps there are some who will say, if this is to
be the issue, let it come. I can have no argument
with those who are prepared to accept, or who wish
for, this issue. All that I know or expect in this
world, of what may be called civil happiness, is
staked on the preservation of our republican consti-

tutional freedom. If others are prepared to yield
it; if others are willing to barter it for the doubly
hazardous experiment of obtaining control over the
destiny of a race not now subject to our sway, or
dependent on our responsibility; if others are ready
to change the foundation of our Union from free
public charters to new authorities obtained by military subjugation — I cannot follow them. I shall
bear that result, if it comes, with such resignation
as may be given to me. But you will pardon me,
fellow-citizens, if, with my humble efforts, I yet
endeavor to sustain those, be they many or few,
who faithfully seek to carry us to the end of these
great perils with the whole system of our civil
liberties unimpaired. You will still, I trust, give
every honest man the freedom to struggle to the
last for that inestimable principle, on which the
very authority of your government to demand the
obedience of all its citizens was founded by those
who created it.

The object for which we are urged by some to
put at imminent hazard the foundation principle of
our Federal system, is, emancipation of the slaves of
the South. No one can be less disposed than myself to undervalue the capacity of my countrymen
to do a great many things — and to do them successfully. One would suppose, however, that a

proposition to effect a sweeping change in the condition of four millions of the laboring peasantry of a great region of country, and to do it in almost total ignorance of the methods in which that particular race can be safely dealt with, so as to produce any good, — would be a proposition upon which even our self-confidence would be likely to pause. One would suppose that such an idea might suggest an inquiry into the limits of human responsibility. It is not allowed among sound moralists, that there is any rule which authorizes a statesman to undo an original wrong, at the imminent hazard of doing another wrong, as great or greater; and there is no rule of moral obligation for a statesman, that is not applicable to the conduct of a people.

Setting aside, then, for a moment, all idea of constitutional restraint, let me put it to each one of you to ask himself how many persons there are in all the North, on whose judgment you would rely for a reasonably safe determination as to what ought to be done with slavery, — having a single view to the welfare of that race? Of course I do not speak of disposing of a few hundred individuals, but of general measures or movements affecting four millions of your fellow-creatures. It has been my fortune, in the course of life, to know a few truly great statesmen in this our Northern latitude, and to know many other persons, for whose general opinions on what concerns the welfare of the human race I should have profound respect. But I have never seen the man, born, educated and living away from contact with slavery as it exists in the South, whom I could regard as competent to determine what radical changes ought to be made in the condition of a race, of whom all that we yet know evinces their present incapacity to become self-sustaining and self-dependent. In such a case, it appears to me a very plain moral proposition, that our Maker has not cast upon us the responsibility of becoming his agents in the premises. But it further appears to me that, in this case, he has surrounded my moral responsibility with other limitations which I cannot transcend. If the order of civil society in which I am placed imposes on me an obligation to refrain from acting on the affairs of others ; if I cannot break that obligation without destroying the principle of a beneficent government and overturning the foundations of property ; if I cannot use the means which I am tempted to employ without danger of unspeakable wrong ; or if the utter inefficacy of those means is apparent to me and to all men, — what is my duty to Him who sets the moral bounds of all my actions ? It is to use those means, and those only, against which He has raised no such gigantic and insuperable moral obstacles. That no valuable military allies can be found among the negroes of the South ; that no description of government custody or charge of them can become more than a change of masters ; and that nothing but weakness to the national cause results from projects that look to the acquisition of national power over their condition, — are truths on which the public mind appears to be rapidly approaching a settled conviction.

I add one word more upon this topic ; and I do it for the purpose of saying in the presence of this community, that any project for arming the blacks against their masters deserves the indignant rebuke of every Christian in the land. When the descendants of those whom Chatham protected against ministerial employment of the Indian scalping-knife, so forget the civilization of the age and their own manhood as to sanction a greater atrocity, we may hang our heads in shame before the nations of the earth.

But there is another aspect of this matter, which it would be entirely wrong to overlook. The great army which has rallied with such extraordinary vigor and alacrity to the defence of the Union and the preservation of the Constitution, — which has endured so much, and has exhibited such heroic

qualities, — is not a standing army of hired merce-
naries. It is an army of volunteers, of citizen sol-
diers who have left their homes and entered the
service of their country, for a special purpose which
they distinctly understood. Permit me to say that
you are bound to remember this ; — or, rather let
me cast aside the language of exhortation, and assert, in your name, that you do remember it with
pride and exultation. The purpose for which these
men were asked to enter the public service was the
protection of the existing Union and the existing
Constitution from attempts to overthrow or change
them by organized violence ; and that purpose is the
most important element in their relation to the
Government. No other army in the world ever entered the service of any power, with an understanding so distinct, so peculiar, so circumscribed in
respect to the objects for which it was to be
used ; so directly addressed to the moral sense and
intelligent judgment of intelligent men. I cannot
doubt that I speak the sentiments of nine men
out of every ten in this community, when I say
that to change that purpose, and to use that army
for any other end than the defence of the Constitution as it is, and the restoration of the Union
of our forefathers, would be a violation of the
public faith.

It is now proposed to enlarge that army by a further call for volunteers. Let them come forth, making no conditions with the Government; for the Government has made its own conditions, and has made them in accordance with the letter and the spirit of the Constitution. The purposes and objects of the war, as declared at the beginning, can never be changed, unless the people shall be so untrue to themselves as to compel a change; and when they do that, they will be themselves responsible for the defeat of their own hopes.

There is yet another topic, on which, as it seems to me, we ought carefully and soberly to reflect. I mean the history of opinion concerning the nature of the Union, and the causes which from time to time have produced disorganizing doctrines respecting it. But let me ask you here not to misunderstand me. I seek no occasion to fasten upon particular persons one or another measure of responsibility for what has occurred; and, therefore, in pursuance of a rule which I have imposed on myself in the preparation of this discourse, the name or designation of no living man, in the North or the South, will pass my lips this day.

Whoever is well acquainted with the political history of this country, since the adoption of the Federal Constitution, must know that there have

been developed at various times, certain strange
opinions concerning the nature of the Federal
Union, the foundation of its authority, and the character of the obligations which we owe to it. In
general, the people of the United States have been
content to rest upon that theory respecting their government which has always prevailed in its official
administration, in whatever hands that administration has been lodged ; — this theory being that the
central government holds certain direct and sovereign, but special, powers over the whole people,
ceded to it by the voluntary grant of the people of
each State. But a sense of injury in certain locali-
ties, springing from wrong supposed to have been
committed or meditated by the ruling majority, or
by those who at the time exercised the power of
the majority, has not infrequently led men here as
elsewhere, to indulge in speculations and acts quite
inconsistent with the only basis on which the government can be said to have any real authority
whatever. To enumerate all these occasions, or to
recite the intemperate conduct that has attended
them in periods of great excitement, is unneces-
sary. But there is one of them, which may serve
as an ample illustration of all that I desire to say
on this special topic.

It is commonly said, — and with much logical

truth, — that the doctrines of Nullification lead, by
natural steps. to the doctrines of Secession ; and
the late Mr. Calhoun, who is justly considered as
the patron. if not the author, of the former, is also
popularly regarded as the father of the latter. But
it is important for us, in more aspects than one
to know that Mr. Calhoun did not contemplate or
desire a dissolution of the Union. He adopted a
doctrine respecting it which does indeed lead, when
consistently followed out, to what is called the constitutional right of secession ; but he did not see
this connection, or intend the consequence. There
is reason to believe that if his confidential corre-
spondence during the times of Nullification shall
ever see the light. it will be found that he was a
sincere lover of the Union, and was wholly uncon-
scious that he was sowing, in the minds of those
who were to come after him, seeds that were to
bear a fatal fruit. It was in his power, at one
time, to have arrested the career of the Nullifiers
in South Carolina, for to them his word was law ;
and if he had so done, he would probably have
been placed by his numerous, powerful, and at-
tached friends, out of that State, in nomination at
least for the highest office in the country.

But what was it that led that subtle, acute and
generally logical intellect to embrace a theory

respecting the Constitution which was entirely at
variance with the facts that attended its establish-
ment? The process was very simple, with a mind
of a highly metaphysical and abstract turn. Mr.
Calhoun had persuaded himself, contrary to an
earlier opinion, that a protective tariff was an unconstitutional exercise of power by the General
Government, oppressive to South Carolina; and he
cast about for a remedy. He saw no relief against
this fancied wrong, likely to come from a majority
of Congress and the people of the Union; and rea-
soning from the premises that the Constitution is a
compact between sovereign *States*, an infraction of
which the parties can redress for themselves when
all other remedy fails, he reached the astounding
conclusion, that the operation of an act of Congress
may be arrested in any State, by a State ordinance,
when that State deems such act an unconstitutional exercise of power. But he always maintained that this was a remedy within the Union,
and not an act of revolution, or violence, or secession.

This memorable example of the mode in which
opinion respecting the nature of our Union is affected, is full of instruction at the present time.
But, let no one misunderstand or misrepresent the
lesson that I draw from it; and, that no one may

have an excuse for so doing, let me be as frank
and explicit as my temporary relation to this audi-
ence demands. I do not say that the course and
result of the late Presidential election furnishes the
least justification or excuse for what the South has
done. I have never believed that any circumstances
of a constitutional election, could of themselves
afford a justification to any State, or any number
of States, in withdrawing from the Union. Neither
do I say, or believe, that any condition of opinion
respecting a right to withdraw, can afford the
slightest apology for that conduct on the part of
individuals, in or out of the government, in respect
to which there must always remain in every sound
mind a great residuum of moral condemnation.
Neither do I doubt at all the existence of a long-
cherished purpose on the part of some Southern
political men, to seize the first pretext for breaking
up the Union of these States.

But, my fellow-citizens, it does appear to me, —
and there is practical importance in the inquiry, in
reference to a future restoration of the Union, —
that we ought soberly to consider, whether any
mere conspiracy of politicians could have found a
*willing people*, if causes had not long been in operation, which have promoted the growth of doctrines

and feelings about the nature and benefits of the Union fatal to its present dominion over their minds and hearts.

What has been going on here in the North during the last twenty or twenty-five years? We have had a faction, or sect, or party, — call it what you will, — constantly increasing, constantly becoming more and more an element in our politics, which has made, not covert and secret, but open and undisguised war upon the Constitution, its authority, its law, and the ministers of its law, because its founders, for wise and necessary purposes, threw the shield of its protection over the institutions of the South. If there is a disorganizing doctrine, or one diametrically hostile to the supremacy of the Constitution, which that faction has not held, inculcated, and endeavored to introduce into public action, I know not where in the whole armory of disunion to look for it. They never cared whether the Constitution was a compact between independent *States*, or an instrument of sovereign government resting on the voluntary grant and stipulation of the people of each State. Destroy it, they said, — destroy it! for, be it one thing or another, it contains that on which the heavens cry out, and against which man ought to rebel. And so they went on doing their utmost to undermine all respect for its obligations, and to render of no kind of importance the foundations on which its authority rests. The more that public men in the North, from weakness, or ambition, or for the sake of party success, assimilated their opinions to the opinions of this faction, the more it became certain that the true ascendancy and supremacy of the Constitution could never be regained, without some enormous exertion of popular energy, following some newly enlightened condition of the popular understanding. When the country was brought to the sharp and sudden necessity of vindicating the nature and authority of the Union, there was throughout the North a general popular ignorance of its real character, and a wide-spread infidelity to some of its important obligations.

What has been going on in the South during the same period? On this point there is much to be learned by those who seek the truth. If you will investigate the facts, you will find that thirty years ago no such opinion as a right of secession had any general acceptance in the South. No general support was given in the South to the conduct of South Carolina, in the matter of nullification. Very few Southern statesmen or politicians of eminence, not belonging to that State, followed Mr. Calhoun

and Mr. Hayne; and when the great debate on
the nature of the Constitution was closed, the
general mind of the South was satisfied with the
result.

How is it now? The simple truth is, that this
great heresy of secession — understood by Southern
politicians as a right resulting from the nature of
the Union — is a growth of the last twenty-five
years; and it has become the prevalent political
faith with the most active of the educated men of
the South who have come into public life during
this period. It is my belief, founded on what I
have had occasion to know, that the great body of
Southern opinion respecting the Constitution, its
nature, its obligations, and its historical basis, has
undergone a complete revolution since the year
1835. What Mr. Calhoun never contemplated as
a remedy against supposed unconstitutional legislation, has become familiar to men's minds as a
remedy against that which was striking deeper than
legislation; which might never take the form of
Congressional action, but was constantly taking
every form of popular agitation; which might
never become the tangible and responsible doctrine
of administration, but was yet all the more for-
midable and irritating, because it lay couched in
an irresponsible popular sentiment, fomented by

appeals which were designed to deprive constitutional ties and obligations of their binding moral force.

Are we told that these things do not stand in any relation of cause and effect? Are we so simple, so uninstructed in what influences the great movements of the human mind, that we cannot see how intellect and passion and interest may be affected by what passes before our eyes? Must I wait until the whole fabric of free constitutional government is pulled down upon my head, and I am buried beneath its ruins, before I cry out in its defence? Must I postpone all judgment respecting the causes of its disintegration, until it has gone down in the ashes of civil war, and History has written the epitaph over the noblest commonwealth that the world has seen? I fear that there is a too prevalent disposition to surrender ourselves as passive instruments into the hands of fate, — too much of abandonment to the current of mere events, — too great a practical denial of our own capacity to save our country by a manly assertion of the moral laws on which its preservation depends. Can it be that we are losing our faith in that Ruler who has made the safety of nations to depend on something more than physical and material strength, who has given us moral power over

our own condition, and has surrounded us with
countless moral weapons for its defence?

It is marvellous through what a course of instruction, through what discipline of suffering and
calamity, the people of this country have had to
pass, in order fully to comprehend the truth that
the nature of their government depends upon sound
deduction from a series of historical facts; and that
it must, therefore, be defended by consistent popular
action. It is now somewhat more than thirty years
since Daniel Webster, combining in himself more
capacities for such a task than had ever been
given to any other American statesman, demonstra-
ted that our national government can have no secure
operation whatever, unless the obviously true and
simple deduction from the facts of its origin is accepted as the basis of its authority. You know
what he taught. You know that he proved — if
ever mortal intellect proved a moral proposition —
that in the exercise of its constitutional powers
the national government is supreme, because every
inhabitant of every State has covenanted with every
inhabitant of every other State that it shall be so;
that even when the national Legislature is supposed
to have overstepped its constitutional limits, no State
interposition, no State Legislation, can afford lawful
remedy or relief; and that all adverse State action,

whether called by the name of Nullification or by
any other name, is unlawful resistance. We are
glad enough now to rest upon his great name ;
we march proudly under his imposing banner, to
encounter the hosts of " constitutional secession."
But how was it with us, even before he was laid
in that unpretending tomb, which rises in the scene
that he loved so well, and overlooks the sounding
sea, by the music of whose billows he went to his
earthly rest? Did we follow in his footsteps? Did
we requite his unequalled civil services? Did we
cherish the great doctrine that he taught us, as the
palladium of a government which must perish if
that doctrine loses its pre-eminence in the national
mind? How long or how well did we preserve the
recollection of his teachings, when our local interests and feelings were arrayed against the action of
the Federal Power? I will not open that record.
I would to Heaven that it were blotted out forever.
But I cannot stand here this day and be guilty of
anything so unfaithful to my country, as to admit
that under a government whose authority can live
only when sustained by popular reverence for
its sanctions and popular belief in its foundations,
opinion in the South has not been affected by what
has transpired in the North.

I have endeavored to state, with fairness and

precision, the principle on which the American Union was founded, and to show that its preservation depends upon keeping the national and the State sovereignties each within the proper limits of its appropriate sphere. I am aware that the opinion has been formed to a great extent in foreign countries and in the South, and by some among us, that this principle is no longer practicable; that the Union of free and slave States in the same nation has become an exploded experiment; and that our interests are so incompatible that a reconstruction, on the old basis at least, ought not to be attempted. We should probably all concede that this view of the subject is correct, if we believed that the incompatibility is necessary, inherent and inevitable. But there is not enough to justify the breaking up of such a union, if the supposed incompatibility is but the result of causes which we can reach, or if it arises from an unfaithful compliance with the terms of our association. We can make such an association no longer practicable if we choose to do so. We can prevent it from becoming impracticable, if we are so resolved. If the free States, as one section, and the slave States as another, will not respect their mutual obligations, then there is an end of the usefulness of all effort. If we, of the North, will not religiously and honestly respect the constitutional right of every State to main-

tain just such domestic institutions as it pleases to
have, and protect that right from every species of
direct and indirect interference, then there is an absolute incompatibility. If they, of the South, will not
as honestly and religiously maintain the right of the
Federal Union to regulate those subjects and interests
which are committed to it by the Constitution, then
there is, in like manner, an incompatibility of pre-
cisely the same nature. If the parties, in reference
to the common domains, will admit of no compromise
or concession, but each insists on applying to them
its own policy as a national policy, then the incompatibility is as complete from that cause as it is from
the others. The difficulty is not in the principle of
the association, for nothing can be clearer than that
principle ; and when it has been honorably adhered
to, no government in the world has worked more
successfully. But the difficulty has arisen from dis-
turbing causes that have dislocated the machine ;
and what we have now to ascertain is, whether the
PEOPLE on both sides will treat those causes as
temporary, and remove them, or will accept them
as inevitable and incurable, and thus make the sep-
aration final and conclusive.

In the gloomy conception of the old Grecian
tragedy, no room was left by the poets for the
moral energies of man, there was no force in

human struggles, no defence in human innocence
or virtue. Higher than Jupiter, higher than the
heavens, in infinite distance, in infinite indifference
to the fortunes of men or gods, sate the mysterious
and eternal power of Destiny. Before time was, its
decrees were made ; and when the universe began,
that awful chancery was closed. No sweet interced-
ing saints could enter there, translated from the
earth to plead for mankind. No angels of love and
mercy came from human abodes, to bring tidings of
their state. No mediator, once a sufferer in the flesh,
stood there to atone for human sin. The wail of a
nation in its agony, or the cry that went up from a
breaking human heart, might pierce into the end-
less realms of space, might call on the elements for
sympathy, but no answer and no relief could come.
He who was pre-ordained to suffer, through whatever agency, suffered and sank, with no consolation
but the thought that all the deities, celestial and
infernal, were alike subject to the same power.

Are we, too, driven by some relentless force, that
annihilates our own free wills and dethrones Him
who is Supreme ? Are we cast helpless and drifting,
like leaves that fall upon the rushing stream? Must
we give way to blank despair? No, no, no! There
are duties to be done—to be done by us : for whatever may be the result of the military struggle now

pending, — whatever may be the effect of victories that have been or shall be won — whatever are to be our future relations with the people of the South, the time is coming when we and they, face to face, and in the eye of an all-seeing God, must determine how we will live side by side as the children of one eternal Parent. For that approaching day, and for the sake of a restoration of that which arms alone cannot conquer, let me implore you to make some fit and adequate preparation of instruments and agents and means and influences. Trust to the humanizing effects of a new and better Intercourse. Trust to the laws of Nature, which have poured through this vast continent the mighty streams that bind us in the indissoluble ties of Commerce. Trust in that Charity — the follower and the handmaid of Commerce — which clothes the naked and feeds the hungry and forgives the erring. Trust in the force of Kindred Blood, which leaps to reconciliation, when the storms of passion are sunk to rest. Trust in that divine law of Love, which has more power over the human soul than all the terrors of the dungeon or the gibbet. Trust in the influence over your own hearts and the hearts of others, of that Religion which was sent as the messenger of Peace on Earth, Good Will to Men. Trust in the wise, beneficent, impartial and neutral spirit of your

Fathers, who gave tranquillity, prosperity and happiness to the whole land. Trust in God: and you may yet see your national emblem, not as the emblem of victory, but as the sign of a reunited American people, floating in the breath of a merciful Heaven, and more radiant with the glory of its restored constellation, than with all the triumphs it has won, or can ever win, over a foreign foe.

www.ingramcontent.com/pod-product-compliance
Lightning Source LLC
Chambersburg PA
CBHW021559270326
41931CB00009B/1293